FINDING-OUT BOOKS

HEAT AND FIRE

by John M. Scott

Illustrations by Lawrence Di Fiori

Parents' Magazine Press — New York

Library of Congress Cataloging in Publication Data

Scott, John Martin, 1913-
    Heat and fire.

    (Finding-out books)
    SUMMARY: Discusses sources and uses of heat and
fire and some solutions for our present energy crisis.
    1. Heat—Juvenile literature.   2. Fire—Juvenile
literature. [1. Heat. 2. Fire]   I. Di Fiori,
Lawrence, illus.   II. Title
QC255.S42   536   73-2813
ISBN 0-8193-0700-9

Contents

4

Chapter One

Gifts from the Sun

Have you ever wondered what it is that makes possible glass in windows, bricks in chimneys, wood in floors, and cement in sidewalks?

The same thing also makes possible the bus you may ride to school, thumbtacks, refrigerators, and man's trip to the moon. And you can use it to make a five-pound block of solid matter vanish completely.

If you have not guessed what we are talking about, here are more hints: it cooks hot dogs, boils water, and helps to grow the radishes and oranges you eat.

It is heat.

Heat melts sand into glass and bakes clay into bricks. Heat from the sun makes trees grow, and trees give us wood. Heat turns a white rock called limestone into cement.

Without heat to melt the red rocks we call iron ore, there would be no steel for automobiles, no refrigerators, no paper clips, no submarines, no bridges.

A jet roars through the sky and a rocket leaps to the moon because of hot gases that rush out of the tailpipe or exhaust port.

An automobile is really a heat engine. In each cylinder of the engine, gasoline, mixed with air, is set on fire by a spark from the spark plug. The heat makes the hot gas expand and push down on the piston. The motion of the piston is carried by the crankshaft and axle to the wheels, and thus the car moves because of heat.

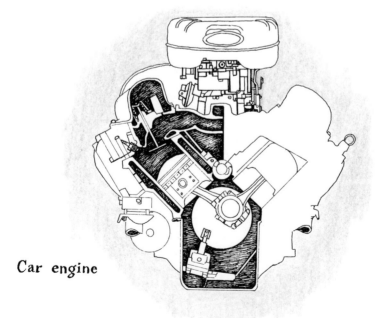

Car engine

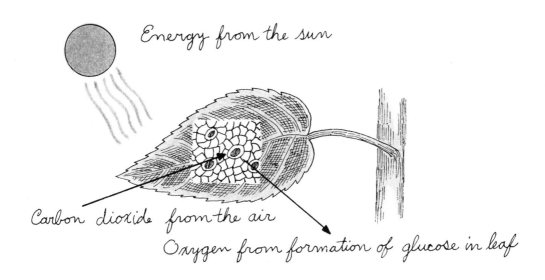

Energy from the sun

Carbon dioxide from the air

Oxygen from formation of glucose in leaf

Almost all the heat we use comes to us, directly or indirectly, from the sun.

Put your hand on the side of your face. The warmth you feel is heat from the sun. You are sun-powered!

The heat of your body comes from the food you eat. Even though an apple or orange may not feel hot, it has a hidden heat called *potential energy*. Energy is the ability to do work. Energy is what makes things go. Potential energy is energy that is stored up. The green leaves of plants take the energy from the sun and store it in the food. When you run, you change the potential, or stored-up energy into *kinetic energy,* or the energy of a moving body.

The next time you pick up a big, kitchen-size match with a wooden stem, think of what you have in your hand. The wood in the match holds energy from the sun hiding and waiting until the golden moment when the match is struck. As soon as the wood starts to burn, the energy from the sun that was stored in the wood will be set free. The heat from the burning wood is energy from the sun that was once captured by leaves on a tree and stored in wood.

Coal, oil, and gas are like the match. They all contain energy captured from the sun.

Oil wells

When ancient swamps and forests were covered
over with deep layers of earth, the trees and plants
buried under the ground were turned to coal. Oil
and gas are the remains of sea animals that once
lived in ancient oceans and got their energy from
plants and seaweeds, which, in turn, took in energy
from the sun. When deep layers of earth covered
over these ancient sea animals, the pressure of the

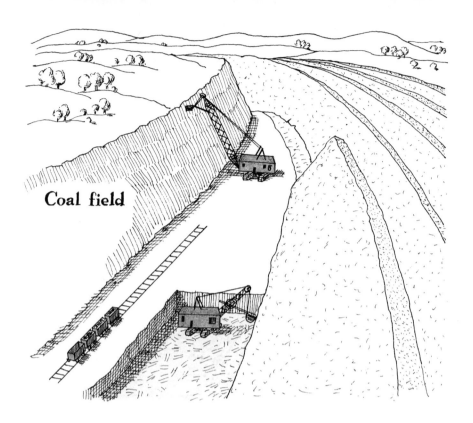

Coal field

earth turned their remains into oil and gas. Thus coal, oil, and gas are gifts from the sun. They are the results of heat.

When we burn coal, we are setting fire to the remains of an ancient forest, and setting free energy from the sun that was held inside the coal for thousands of years.

Can you now tell why coal is called "black sunlight"? And why oil is called "liquid sunlight"?

Chapter Two

How Hot Is It?

Heat is a form of energy caused by the motion of molecules. Everything on earth is made of tiny bits called molecules. A molecule of salt is the tiniest bit of salt. A molecule of water is the tiniest bit of water.

The faster the molecules in a thing move, the hotter it gets. The difference between a hamburger just out of a refrigerator and one just out of a frying pan is that the molecules in the cooked hamburger are moving faster.

The molecules in your chair, your pencil, or in your shoes are always in motion. If we could look into this tiny world of molecules, we would find motion everywhere. The heat energy contained in any body is the sum of all the energy in all its many

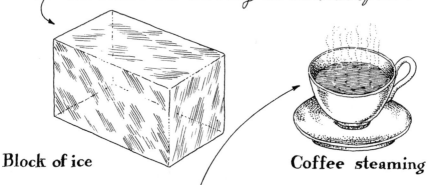

These molecules are moving the slowest of all.

Block of ice　　　　　　**Coffee steaming**

The molecules in this liquid are moving fast

molecules. Things that we call cold are objects that have less heat than other objects.

Things get bigger, or expand, when they are heated, because heat makes molecules move. When an object is heated its molecules speed up, bang into each other harder, and push each other farther apart.

To find out how heat makes molecules move faster, put some water in a teakettle and place it on the stove. When the water gets hot, some of the molecules will move fast enough to leap out of the water and jump out of the spout as steam.

You cannot see steam. But when steam meets

These molecules are moving still faster

the air some of its molecules lose their heat and become liquid once more. It is condensed steam, or vapor, in the form of fine bits or particles of water that you see and call steam.

There is usually a clear space between the spout of a boiling teakettle and the cloud of condensing steam. In this clear space is the real, invisible steam.

When one pound of water turns into one pound of steam it expands, or grows about 1,700 times larger. Heat does not make the molecules of water any larger, but it speeds them up so that they hit each other harder, and move farther apart after hitting.

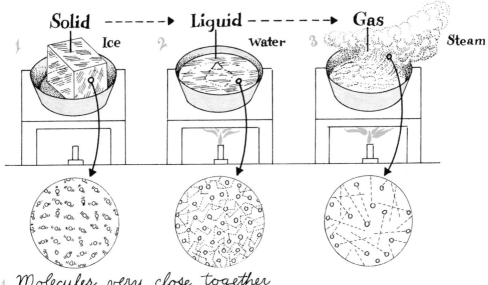

Solid ------▶ **Liquid** -------▶ **Gas**

Ice   Water   *Steam*

1 *Molecules very close together*
2 *Molecules move faster and are farther apart*
3 *Molecules move even faster and spread out*

Why is it that you cannot walk through a block of ice, but can walk through a puddle of water? It is because of the form of the molecules, and this form is determined by heat.

In a block of ice, which is water in a solid state, the molecules have so little heat that they are very close together. Trying to walk through them would be like trying to walk through a group of one hundred people standing shoulder to shoulder and tightly holding hands.

You can walk through a puddle because the
molecules of water in the liquid state have more
heat and, therefore, move faster and are farther
apart. It would be like walking through a big
supermarket where one hundred people are scattered
all over the store. The people are far enough apart
so that you can walk through the crowd.

If you were standing by the stove while someone was frying bacon, what would hurt you most—to have one drop of hot grease fall on you, or to have all the grease in the frying pan spill on you?

You will probably answer: "One drop of grease would not hurt me as much as all the grease."

But why not? Don't they both have the same temperature?

They do both have the same temperature, but the amount of grease in the drop is so small that it does not have much heat. There are more molecules in the grease in the frying pan, so all together they would have more heat.

As we have said, the energy of motion is called kinetic energy. Temperature is a measure of the speed, or kinetic energy, of single molecules. The more rapid the rate of motion of molecules, the higher the temperature.

But temperature does not tell how much heat any one person or thing has. A gallon of boiling water has the same temperature as a quart of boiling water, but the gallon has four times the heat of the quart because it has four times as many molecules.

What has more heat—a cup of steaming hot coffee or the Hudson River on a cold day in winter?

The separate molecules in the coffee are moving very fast, so they have a high temperature. The

molecules in the cold river are moving slowly, so
they have a lower temperature. But there are many
millions of times as many molecules in the river as
there are in the cup. For that reason, all of the river
molecules taken together will have more heat than
the coffee.

A Fourth-of-July sparkler is a good example of the difference between heat and temperature. A warning stamped on the side of the sparkler box says: "Danger. Do Not Touch Glowing Wire."

Why will the glowing wire burn your hand while the glowing sparks won't?

Even though the glowing wire and the sparks have the same temperature, the sparks have little heat because they are so small. They have little mass, or weight. The wire has more heat, even though it has the same temperature, because it has more mass, more weight. There is more material in it.

How can we measure the temperature of a body?
How can we tell how fast the molecules of anything
are moving?

To prove that no one can just guess what the
temperature is, try the following experiment:

Place three pans on the table. Fill the first with
cold water and ice cubes. Put lukewarm water in the
second pan. And fill the third pan with water as hot
as you can stand. *Be sure it isn't hot enough to
burn you.*

Place your left hand in the ice water and your
right hand in the hot water. After keeping your
hands in the pans for about two minutes, place both
hands in the lukewarm water. Your right hand will
tell you that the water is cool. Your left hand will
tell you that the water is hot. Neither is true. Now

Cold water   Hot water   Lukewarm water

you know why we need thermometers that do not depend on our senses.

The common thermometer is made of a slim glass tube with a bulb at the bottom. The bulb is usually filled with mercury. Sometimes alcohol, or some other liquid, such as toluene, is used.

Since molecules move faster and spread farther apart when heated, the mercury increases in volume and rises in the tube when the temperature is high. It may be marked with the Fahrenheit scale, abbreviated F., or with the centigrade scale, abbreviated C. In weather reports temperatures are given on the Fahrenheit scale. Scientists use the centigrade scale.

Do you know what zero means on your thermometer?

In 1724, when Gabriel Fahrenheit invented the thermometer that now bears his name, the coldest temperature that could be obtained experimentally was reached by mixing equal parts of salt with ice or snow. Fahrenheit decided to call this temperature zero. If you have ever helped make homemade ice

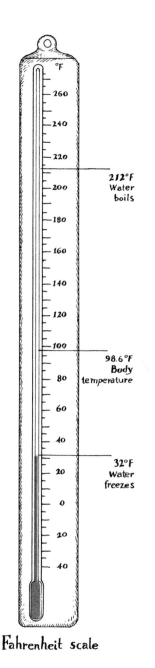

°F

260

240

220

212°F
Water
boils

200

180

160

140

120

100

98.6°F
Body
temperature

80

60

40

32°F
Water
freezes

20

0

20

40

Fahrenheit scale

cream, you may have poured salt into the pail of ice to get the temperature down to zero.

Fahrenheit put the 100-degree mark on his thermometer to equal what he thought to be the normal temperature of a healthy human body. Later, more accurate measurements found that the body temperature is usually 98.6 degrees.

On the Fahrenheit scale the temperature at which water freezes is 32 degrees. Water boils at 212 degrees. The temperature at which water freezes and the temperature at which water boils are known as the fixed points on the thermometer.

How is a reliable, accurate thermometer made?

The glass tube is first examined to be sure that the hollow center is the same size along the entire length of the tube. A bulb is blown at one end, and mercury is put into the tube. The bulb is then gently heated to push out the air. The mercury rises in the tube, and when it reaches the top this end of the tube is sealed off over a hot flame. As the liquid in the tube cools and shrinks, it leaves an almost perfect vacuum—an empty space where there is no air—above it. The tube is now ready to mark.

The tube is first put into a mixture of ice and water. As the mercury cools, it shrinks and falls. When it stops falling, a short line, showing the freezing point of water, is marked on the tube. This is 32 degrees on the Fahrenheit scale. The tube is

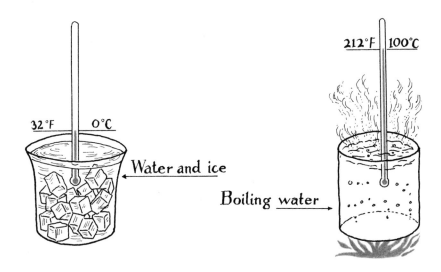

32 °F   0 °C

Water and ice

212°F   100°C

Boiling water

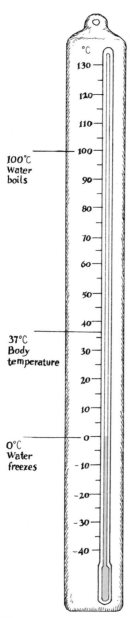

°C

130

120

110

100 — 100°C Water boils

90

80

70

60

50

40

30 — 37°C Body temperature

20

10

0 — 0°C Water freezes

-10

-20

-30

-40

Centigrade scale

now put in a steam bath above boiling water. The mercury rises to its greatest height. A second mark is made on the glass to show the boiling point, 212 degrees on the Fahrenheit scale. The space between 32 and 212 degrees is divided into 180 equal units, or marks. Each mark stands for one degree.

In 1742 Anders Celsius, a Swedish astronomer, invented a thermometer using the centigrade scale. On the centigrade scale, zero is considered as the temperature at which water freezes. The boiling point of water is 100 degrees. On the centigrade scale there are 100 degrees between the freezing and boiling points of water.

24

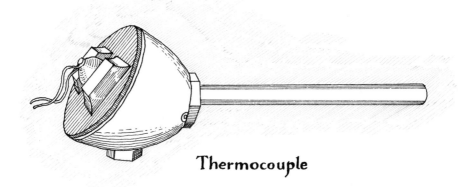

Thermocouple

To measure very high or very low temperatures, scientists use special instruments such as thermocouples, optical pyrometers, bolometers, and temperature sensors.

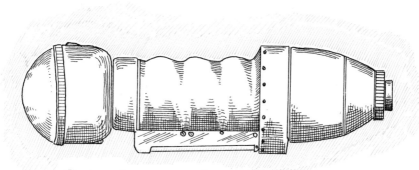

Optical pyrometer

Mercury is a metal that is in the liquid state at room temperature. Its freezing point is minus 39 degrees Fahrenheit and its boiling point is about 672 degrees. One advantage of alcohol is that its freezing point is minus 179 degrees Fahrenheit. At Rogers Pass in Montana, temperatures drop to minus 70 degrees Fahrenheit. At this temperature a mercury thermometer would be frozen solid, but an alcohol thermometer would still work. Also, alcohol can be colored by adding red or blue dyes, which makes it easier to read the degree of temperature. There is no satisfactory way to color mercury.

Chapter Three

Turn on the Heat

How can you make things hot?

Since heat depends on the motion of the molecules, you can heat a thing by getting its molecules to move faster. Rub your hands together and notice how warm they become. That is because of *friction,* a word that comes from a Latin word meaning "to rub."

If you make a mistake while writing a letter, and then use an eraser, note how friction warms both the eraser and the paper.

Basketball players sometimes stumble and slide across the hardwood floor in a gym and get a "floor burn." Indians once started fires by rubbing two sticks together. If ever you made the mistake of trying to pick up and hold on to a rope with your bare hands while someone was pulling it across the floor, you may have had a very painful rope burn. You light a match by dragging it across a rough surface.

Dentists' drills cause friction and that is why they are unpleasant. The friction is caused by the spinning drill, which makes heat. To get rid of this heat, many dental drills have water sprays that shoot cold water on the tooth while it is being drilled.

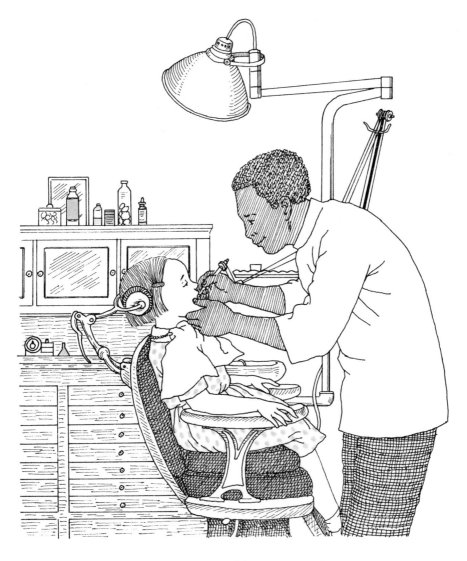

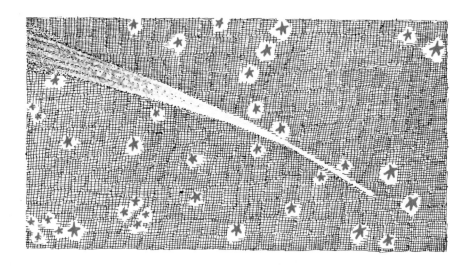

If you wish to see an object shooting through the air so fast that it catches fire, just look up into the sky at night. If you are lucky, you may see a shooting star.

A shooting star is not a star at all. It is a hard lump of metal and stone that rushes in from outer space at a speed of about forty miles a second. Friction between the fast-moving rock and our air sets it on fire. What you see is the white-hot burning trail of gas formed by friction. The high heat of friction burns the rock to ashes within about ten miles. Each day some two tons or more of these ashes fall on the earth.

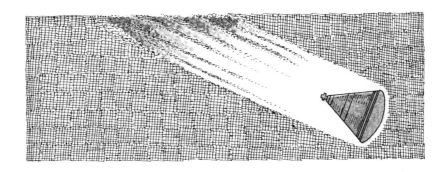

When our Apollo astronauts came back from the moon, their spacecraft slammed into the air over our heads at 24,700 miles an hour. Friction caused the heat to build up to 5,000 degrees Fahrenheit.

Another way to make heat is by pressure.

Get two ice cubes and hold one in each hand with a towel to keep your hands from getting too cold. Place the ice cubes so that they are face to face and press hard. If you can press hard enough, the ice cubes will melt where their faces, or surfaces, touch. When you take your hands and the towel away, the layer of water between the ice cubes will freeze, and the cubes will stick together.

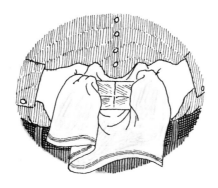

When you make snowballs you squeeze the snow to make enough heat to melt some of it. When you stop pressing, the water in the snow will freeze, leaving a firm snowball.

When you skate on ice, the pressure of your skate melts the ice and forms a thin film of water over which the skate moves. You are really skating on water. When you lift up your foot, the water freezes immediately.

Entrance to Kelley mine

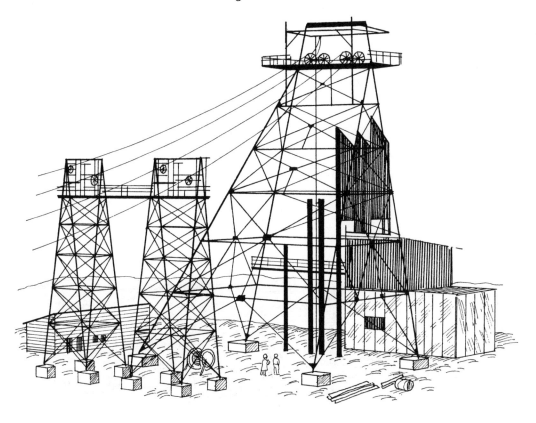

Pressure makes it warm inside the earth. In some
mines the temperature goes up one degree for every
sixty feet the miners go into the earth. In the
copper city of Butte, Montana, the Kelley mine has
a shaft, or hole, that goes down almost one mile
into the earth. The temperature of the rock at this
depth is 150 degrees Fahrenheit.

In Wyoming there are oil wells that go down to 20,521 feet. The temperature at this depth is 400 degrees Fahrenheit.

Heat can be made by collision, or by hitting or banging. Use a hammer to pound a nail into a block of wood. Then put your finger on the head of the nail, and you'll find it is warm. In South Dakota, many years ago, two trains going at high speeds hit head on. So great was the heat made by the collision that some parts on the fronts of both engines were melted together.

You can heat a wire by bending it back and forth rapidly. The wire gets hot because you make its molecules move.

If you ever pumped air into a bicycle tire, a football, or a basketball, did you notice how warm the bottom of the hand pump got? This heat is due not only to the friction of the plunger inside the

tube or piston, but also to the fact that you
compress, or squeeze, air molecules into a
small space.

Pushing a great number of air molecules into a
smaller space is like chasing wild horses into a small
corral, or yard. So many galloping horses are pushed
into a small space that they are always bumping
into the sides of the corral and hitting the fence.

35

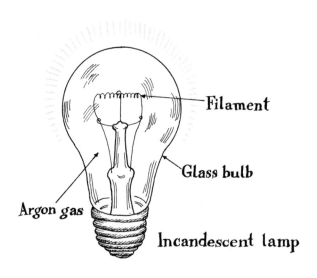

Filament

Glass bulb

Argon gas

Incandescent lamp

The more horses you push into a corral, the more often the walls or the fence will be hit by flying hoofs and thumping bodies.

Electricity can make heat. The next time you plug in an electric toaster, or turn on an electric stove, notice how the coils become red and glow.

Do you know why the light bulbs in your home are called incandescent lamps? The word "incandescent" means "glowing white-hot." And this is exactly what happens. The electricity going through the very thin wires, or filaments, in the lamps makes them glow white-hot, so they give off light as well as heat.

Do you know that every day a big explosion is taking place over your head?

Although the sun is not exactly a hydrogen bomb, it works something like one. A great part of the sun is made of a gas called hydrogen. Each second some four million tons of the sun's mass, or matter, is completely changed into energy—heat and light that dash away from the sun in all directions at the speed of 186,000 miles in a second. But scientists tell us that, even so, there is enough hydrogen in the sun to last for billions of years. Planet Earth gets only one part in two billion of this energy given off by the sun.

So far we have spoken only of molecules. But there are even smaller things than molecules. They are called atoms, and they are the smallest particles we know. A molecule of water, for example, has two atoms of hydrogen and one of oxygen. Atoms are sometimes called the building blocks of the universe. There are over one hundred different kinds.

Even though the atom is very small, it is made of parts. The inside, or center, of an atom is called the *nucleus.* When the nucleus turns into energy, we have a very great amount of heat.

MOLECULE

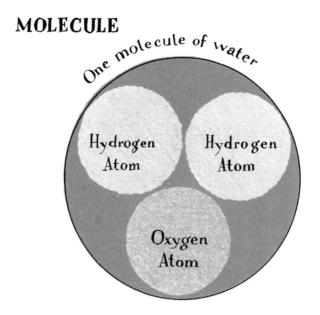

One molecule of water

Hydrogen Atom

Hydrogen Atom

Oxygen Atom

Because the change from matter to energy takes place in the nucleus of the hydrogen atoms in the sun, the heat given off is said to come from nuclear energy.

Although nuclear energy is an old story with the sun, it was not until this century that scientists found out why the sun is so hot. Once man knew the secret of the sun, he could control nuclear energy, and use it for man's benefit.

What do you think would happen to our planet if we were ten times closer to the sun than we are now?

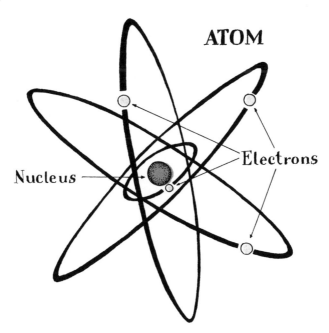

ATOM

Nucleus

Electrons

Chapter Four

Fire

What is it that our great-grandparents used to cook their meals and to warm their homes in winter—yet this same thing sometimes turned a house into ashes, and killed?

The thing they used every day but had to be careful to control was heat from chemical energy or fire.

Look at a burning match. The fire you see occurs because fuel (wood) has combined, or united, with the oxygen in the air so fast that heat and light are given off.

Instead of saying that the match is burning, we could say that it is oxidizing, or uniting with oxygen. When fuel unites with oxygen, the process is called *oxidation.*

Sometimes the joining of the fuel with the oxygen is so slow that no heat is noticed. Rust is the result of slow oxidation. If you have an old iron gate that is rusting or an iron frying pan in the kitchen that gets rusty, you know that the iron is uniting with the oxygen in the air.

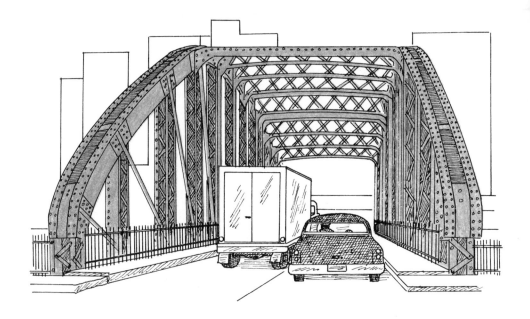

Do you know why we paint cars, steel bridges, and tractors? The layer of paint keeps the steel from uniting with the oxygen in the air.

Decay, or rotting, is another form of slow oxidation. The refrigerator in your home keeps food from oxidizing. When it is very cold, molecules are too inactive, or slow, to combine with oxygen. Perhaps you never thought of it this way, but the job of the refrigerator is to keep the molecules inside the box from moving too quickly.

Even a cup of kerosene cannot be lit with a match if the kerosene is ice-cold. If you live in the

North, you know that cars may be hard to start on cold mornings.

The temperature at which each kind of fuel will start to unite with oxygen is called the *ignition point*. It is different for different fuels.

One fuel is phosphorus. It has such a very low ignition point that it will start to burn at room temperature. On the other hand, some things we don't think of as fuels will burn if the heat is great enough.

By now you can see that three things are needed to make a fire—fuel, oxygen, and heat. Take away any one of these things, and the fire will stop. To fight fire we have to take away one or more of these three things.

Here is a way to find out that oxygen is needed for fire. Get an old ketchup bottle, or any bottle of about that size and shape. Wash it out carefully. Now roll a little strip of paper around a pencil. Pull the pencil out, and light one end of the paper with a match. Be sure to use a long kitchen match so you don't burn your fingers. As soon as the paper is burning brightly, drop it into the bottle. See how fast the burning paper uses up the oxygen in the bottle. As soon as the oxygen is used up, the fire goes out.

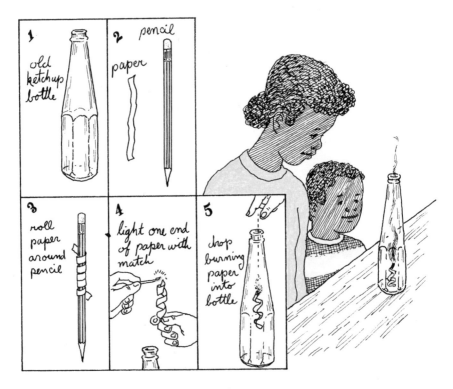

Next Hallowe'en when you turn a pumpkin into a jack-o-lantern, light a candle inside it; then put the top back on the pumpkin. See how dimly the candle is burning. Now take the top off the pumpkin. Why does the candle burn brightly again?

Hold a glass tumbler upside down over a candle flame. The smaller the glass, the sooner the flame goes out. The reason is that the smaller glass has less air and so less oxygen.

We throw sand on campfires and cover burning grease on the stove with a pan lid for the same reason—to cut off the supply of oxygen.

The big cardboard boxes in which matches are sent to stores may have this sign printed on them in large letters: "IF THIS BOX STARTS TO SMOKE, DO NOT BREAK OPEN. LEAVE THE BOX CLOSED AND THE FIRE WILL GO OUT." By now you know why. The fire will soon use up the oxygen in the box. Once the oxygen is gone, the fire will go out.

If you hold a glowing match to a block of wood, the wood does not burst into flame. But if the block is cut into very small pieces or splinters, or made into shavings, the splinters and shavings will burn easily. That is because the pile of shavings allows more surfaces of the wood to be exposed to the air.

You can even burn iron, if you expose enough of
its surface to the oxygen in the air. To see how this
works, pick up a wad of steel wool with a pair of
tongs and hold the steel wool over a candle flame.
Be very careful not to get too close to it. The
sparkling "stars" of burning steel wool you will see
come from tiny bits of steel uniting with the
oxygen.

The more surface a fuel offers to the air, the faster
it will burn. Coal is often powdered, then blown
into a furnace. In a big diesel engine, like those on
trains and busses, the fuel oil is sprayed through a
nozzle that breaks the stream of oil up into a mist.

Coal dust in a mine can lead to a terrible
explosion. Even flour and cornmeal will burn if they
get enough air. That is why men working in grain

elevators and cargo ships take special care to keep
dust from building up. If the temperature is high
enough, the fuel will burst into flame. Even
powdered lead, when shaken into the air from a test
tube or container, will break into flame when the
temperature of the room is high enough.

This kind of burning is called *spontaneous combustion.*

A flash bulb for taking indoor pictures gives us a
good example of the three things that are needed to
make heat or fire:

Look inside the glass bulb and you will see fine threads of aluminum or magnesium. This is the fuel. The metal is shredded so as to expose the greatest possible surface to the oxygen.

You cannot see the oxygen, but it is there. It fills the bulb and surrounds the fine pieces of shredded metal.

A spark from a battery sets off the flash bulb. This causes the heat. The oxygen unites so rapidly with the metal that there is one great flash of light and heat.

Now look at an ordinary light bulb, such as you use in a lamp. If you have a bulb with clear glass, you can see the filament. (See picture, page 36.) Notice that the filament is *not* shredded, but is made of a piece of solid wire. The most important thing is something you cannot see. There is *no* oxygen in the bulb. All the air was taken out to keep the filament from burning up. A gas called argon was then put into the bulb. This gas does not

Edison's first bulb

burn. Instead, it acts like a blanket around the filament to keep it from boiling and going into a vapor. When you turn on a lamp, a lot of electricity is going through the filament, but the wire does not burn up because there is no oxygen in the bulb.

Thomas Edison knew that many scientists before him had made some sort of light with electricity, but the filaments burned up too fast. Edison got the idea of putting the filament into a glass bulb from which the air could be removed. His idea worked. In 1879 he invented the first practical incandescent lamp, or light bulb. The main thing Edison did that scientists before him failed to do was to take the oxygen away from the filament.

Edison's workshop

Although Edison's lamp worked, the filament in the vacuum turned little by little into a gas, or vapor, which hit the inside of the glass bulb and darkened it.

In 1912, another scientist, Dr. Irving Langmuir, put argon gas inside the bulb. This not only made the filament last longer, but also kept the bulb from blackening so fast. Argon gas is called *inert* because it does not unite with things the way oxygen does.

One way to control a fire is to remove the fuel, if possible. This method is sometimes used in fighting forest fires. Trees are cut down ahead of the fire. When the fire reaches the cut-down area, there is no fuel, and it burns out.

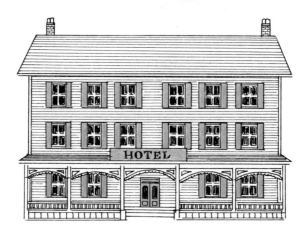

Many years ago, hotels were made with wooden floors, wooden walls, and wooden steps. The curtains in the hotel were made of cloth that caught fire easily. As we have seen, one way to control a fire is to remove the fuel. Modern hotels do just that. Instead of wood, they have cement floors, brick walls, and cement or steel steps. They may have curtains made of a glass material that does not burn.

One of the most common methods of controlling fires is that used by most fire departments. They use water to cool the fuel to the

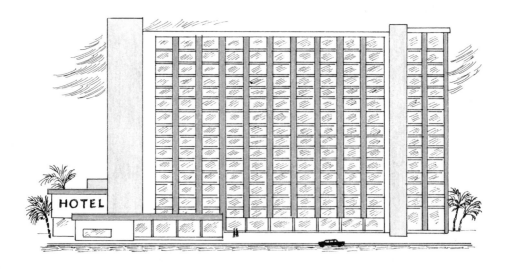

point where it will no longer burn. The great streams of water leaping from the fire hoses not only rob the fuel of the needed heat, but also smash down on the burning area to smother the flames and block the air from them. In addition, as the water turns to steam, it takes in great amounts of heat. Thus, the fuels may be cooled below their ignition point.

You may have noticed that when a big building is burning close to other buildings, firemen keep spraying water on the roofs of the nearby buildings to keep them cool.

Most forest fires take place in the summer. The fire lookout stations in many forests are closed during the winter months, since cold weather and snow help to keep the wood in the trees from reaching a temperature at which it can start burning.

What was the biggest thing ever to sail through the sky between Europe and the United States?

It was the giant, cigar-shaped balloon, or dirigible, called the *Hindenburg*. The huge airship was filled with hydrogen gas, which is highly explosive. On May 6, 1937, as the *Hindenburg* moved toward its mooring post at Lakehurst, New Jersey, the hydrogen gas united with the oxygen in the air in the presence of a spark. The great explosion destroyed the *Hindenburg* and killed thirty-six people.

Remember: NEVER use a lighted match to look into an empty gasoline can. The drops of gasoline still left in the can turn to a vapor, or gas, and mix with the oxygen in the air to make a most powerful

explosive. All it needs is the heat from a match to make it go into action.

Thirty-one years after the *Hindenburg* explosion, a Saturn 5 rocket leaped to the moon from Cape Kennedy. The fuel that pushed the rocket into the sky was hydrogen!

The man who learned how to work safely with hydrogen was America's greatest rocket expert, Dr. Wernher von Braun, who is known as the "Father of the Saturn." He is given as much credit for learning to work with hydrogen as he is for making the Saturn.

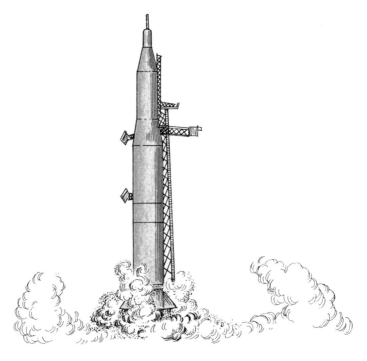

Chapter Five

What About the Future?

We have been using coal, gas, and oil (known as fossil fuels) so rapidly that scientists and the government are getting worried. Our own natural resources are running out, and we are bringing in more and more oil from other countries, which means it costs more. Besides, the other countries may begin to have shortages, too.

Scientists around the world are working to help solve this energy crisis. Here in the United States many new nuclear power plants are now being built to produce electricity by using energy from uranium. But these often kill the fish in the waters near them, and no one is entirely sure that they are safe.

In Sonoma County, California, is America's first

Turbine

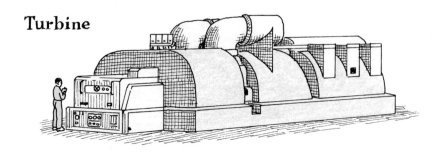

geothermal power plant. "Geo" means earth, and "thermal" means hot. This "hot earth" power plant captures hot steam that comes out of the ground and uses it to spin turbines that make electricity. A turbine is a machine that looks something like a windmill with fan-like blades. When hot steam hits the blades on the turbine, it turns an axle connected to coils of wire that spin between magnets. This makes electricity. A turbine may also be turned by water.

The street lights of Paris are now turned on by the ocean's tides—not directly, of course, but in this unusual way: Twice a day the tides race up the Rance River to raise the water level as high as 44 feet, so engineers built a big dam to trap the water, and let it run through turbines to make electricity.

High up in the mountains of France a giant mirror catches the sun's light like a magnifying

glass. It produces a temperature of more than 6,000 degrees Fahrenheit, enough to melt almost anything on earth.

The sun, as we said at the beginning, is the greatest energy source of all. Some day in the next century we may capture energy from the sun by giant satellites in space. This energy could then be sent to planet Earth in much the same way we send radio waves today.

But in the meantime we must make do with what we have, and not waste it. Some states are thinking about an extra tax that would make people use less gas and electricity. Builders are thinking about putting up buildings that will need less heating.

We can all help by stopping to think, so we don't turn on a light, or the television set, for example, and then walk out of the room. Even the companies that make money by selling us energy are now asking us to use as little as we can.

Can you think of other ways to save energy?

Index